Halloween Book of Fun

Puzzles, Games, Jokes, Ideas, and More

Edited by Jeffrey A. O'Hare

Boyds Mills Press

Published by Bell Books
Boyds Mills Press, Inc.
A Highlights Company
815 Church Street
Honesdale, Pennsylvania 18431
Printed in China

U.S. Cataloging-in-Publication Data
(Library of Congress Standards)

Halloween book of fun : puzzles, games, jokes, ideas, and more
/ edited by Jeffrey A. O'Hare.—1st ed.
[64]p. : col. ill. ; cm.
Summary: Puzzles, games, and other activities with a Halloween theme.
ISBN 1-56397-959-4
1. Halloween. 2. Puzzles. 3. Games. 4. Riddles. I. O'Hare, Jeffrey A.
II. Title.
394.2646 21 2001 CIP AC

First edition, 2001
Book designed by Randy Llewellyn
The text of this book is set in New Century Schoolbook.

10 9 8 7 6 5 4 3 2 1

Pumpkin Picking

How many pumpkins can you pick from this picture?

Illustrated by Tom Powers

Monster Mash

It's time for the annual Horrible Hoedown at Castle Karloff. As an added party favor, our host has posted this coded riddle. Use the key to figure out what each symbol means and to decipher the secret message.

Why do grave diggers make excellent storytellers?

Answer on page 62

Illustrated by Jeff Shelly

Row, Row, Row

Each of the partygoers below is wearing a costume that has something in common with the two others in the same row. For example, in the top row across, each person is wearing something green. Look at the other rows across, down, and diagonally. Can you tell what each row has in common?

Illustrated by Frank Bolle

Answer on page 62

Don't Be Afraid

The words in this list are associated with October 31. First find and circle all of them in the grid, either across, up, down, backward, or diagonally. Then darken in all the letters found in HALLOWEEN that were not part of any word you circled. When done correctly, a picture will appear.

- BAG
- BATS
- BLACK
- BOO
- BREW
- BROOMS
- CANDY
- CATS
- COSTUMES
- CREEPY
- FUN
- GHOSTS
- GHOULS
- GOBLINS
- GOOD
- HALLOWEEN
- HAT
- HOWL
- MASK
- MONSTERS
- MOON
- NIGHT
- ORANGE
- PUMPKINS
- SCARY
- SCREAM
- TRICK OR TREAT
- WITCHES
- WOLF

B	G	O	T	R	I	C	K	O	R	T	R	E	A	T
G	H	O	U	L	S	E	M	U	T	S	O	C	C	J
G	O	B	L	I	N	S	U	A	J	W	O	L	F	K
O	S	C	A	R	Y	I	L	Z	Y	P	E	E	R	C
O	T	B	N	E	W	T	O	R	H	L	A	R	G	A
D	S	L	V	B	C	O	L	W	U	D	X	E	B	L
S	H	C	A	N	D	Y	M	A	E	R	C	S	E	B
N	W	G	E	O	M	A	S	K	L	E	F	M	E	S
I	A	S	G	N	E	T	Y	W	E	L	T	O	A	R
K	O	T	N	E	E	W	O	L	L	A	H	O	O	E
P	L	A	A	E	I	H	A	P	H	N	G	R	L	T
M	E	B	R	C	L	F	U	N	H	Z	I	B	H	S
U	T	O	O	C	N	W	A	L	H	V	N	E	J	N
P	B	C	L	S	E	H	C	T	I	W	E	M	C	O
S	T	A	C	H	A	N	H	A	E	N	N	O	O	M

Answer on page 62

Illustrated by Tom Powers

Monster Mansion

Twelve of the most famous movie monsters of all time are hidden in this scary scene. How many can you find?

Illustrated by Joe Seidita

Ghostly Gags

Monster Mouth

To get a monster mouth, cut an orange or grapefruit into four equal pieces. Peel the skin off one section. Now ask an adult to help you cut a jagged line in the center of the peel, without reaching the ends. Next, put the peel in your mouth with the white side facing away from you. Use your tongue to push the new "teeth" out at weird angles. You can even stick your tongue out through the slice for a better effect.

Spooky Sounds

Have you ever wanted to haunt your own house? Here's how to do it. First, get a tape recorder. Let the tape run for one or two minutes before you begin recording scary sounds. That way, when people look around to see what's making all the noise, you'll have already moved across the room, away from the recorder.

Now, what noises should you put on this tape? Screams and moans are scary, but if you want to be even more terrifying, try these:

1. To get the sound of chains clanking, rattle some empty cans together.

2. Look around the house for the creakiest door. If you can't find a door, try a creaky board on the floor. Make it creak slowly, and record the noise a few times. Then play the creaks back loudly.

3. A howling wind can be created by blowing across the top of a soda bottle.

4. People will think they're being attacked by giant bugs if you crush some cereal, like wheat squares, over and over. Have a friend move the recorder closer each time you crush the cereal, so the munching gets louder and louder. Everyone else will run from the approaching bugs.

Put the recorder someplace out of sight when you start it. When the noises begin (after the one- or two-minute wait), remember to act as scared as all your friends.

Scary Slime

Mix these ingredients in a big bowl: four tablespoons of flour, two teaspoons of salt, a drop of olive oil, a few drops of food coloring, and two tablespoons of water. Use your hands to mix all these ingredients together, adding more flour or water if necessary. (The mixture should be squishy, but not too sticky.) Sculpt the slime into scary monsters of all shapes and sizes. Add plastic eyes or chenille stick antennae. Leave your creatures to dry in a warm place, or ask an adult to bake them in an oven at a low temperature. When they are dry, paint them in scary colors.

Illustrated by Terry Sirrell

Peter, Peter, Pumpkin Poser

Peter proudly presents his prize pumpkins. All but one of these jolly jack-o'-lanterns matches another jack-o'-lantern. Can you find all the pairs of pumpkins? Then try to find a match for the one leftover jack-o'-lantern.

Illustrated by Lynn Adams

Answer on page 62

Mummy's the Word

After a rough four-thousand-year sleep, these mummies awoke to find themselves a bit knotted. Can you match which scepter belongs to which mummy by untangling the wrappings?

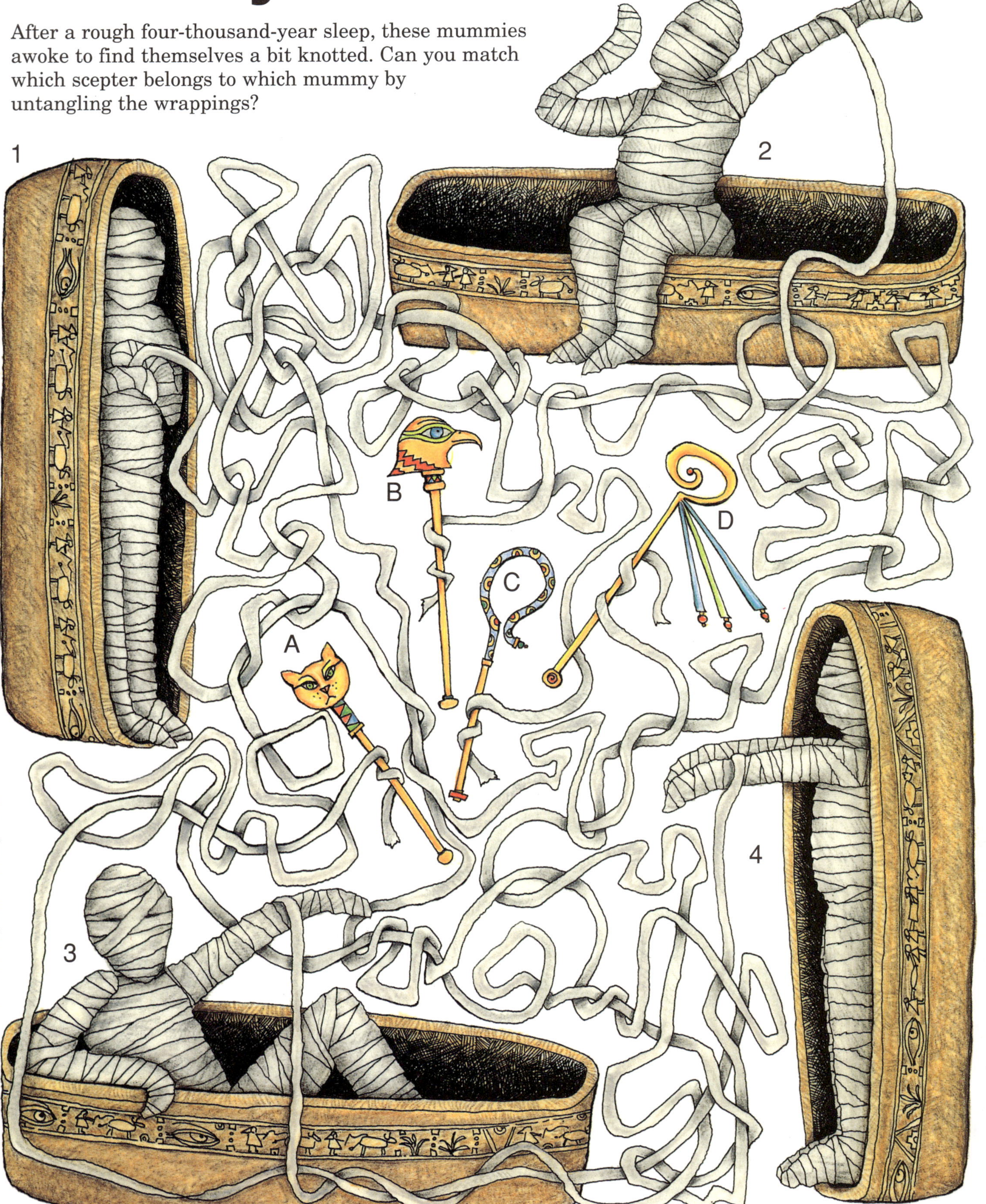

Illustrated by Liisa Chauncy Guida

Answer on page 62

What's in a Word?

On Halloween, children go out for goodies. But did you ever notice all the "goodies" hiding in the letters of HALLOWEEN, such as HALL? There are at least thirty-five words of three letters or more masked here. Don't be tricked. Get a treat by seeing how many words you can find in HALLOWEEN.

Answer on page 62

Illustrated by Anni Matsick

Tube Test

Dr. Karloff has lost all his test tubes. How many can you find?

Look and See

The words for many of the items in this scene end in double letters, such as TREE and DOLL. How many such things do you see?

Illustrated by Bill Basso

Conga Din

The Puzzle Pals found a great way to break the ice with their party guests. As these conga lines hit full swing, see if you can find all the differences between the two pictures.

Illustrated by Tim Ellis

House-to-House

Be careful as you look through this large picture to find the iron, clothespin, flashlight, wristwatch, teacup, telephone receiver, pencil, owl, knitted cap, lollipop, loaf of bread, slice of cake, sock, and cat.

Illustrated by R. Michael Palan

Fright Sights

Oh no! Professor Hink Pink's search to find rhymes has taken him into this haunted house. Now his ghost host is showing off all the scary things that rhyme. How many rhymes can you find in these fright sights?

Answer on page 62

Illustrated by Terry Rogers

Lost in the Castle

You are exploring a mysterious castle. In front of you are five numbered doors. Only one of the doors leads out of the castle. The other doors must not be opened, or the flying Giant Lintax, who has slept for the past three hundred years, will escape and you will be trapped in the castle for the next three hundred years.

Scratched on the wall is this clue. Can you solve the puzzle and escape the castle?

Illustrated by Bill Colrus

A Prize Pumpkin

This pumpkin won the prize for the most unusual jack-o'-lantern. But why is it so unusual? Is it purple or green? Does it have a funny face or a big mustache? Use your imagination to draw in and color what you think this pumpkin looks like.

Illustrated by Bill Colrus

CAT & DOG MYSTERY

CASE # 222
The Haunted Library

"Be careful," Jason Jackal warned as he carefully pushed open the doors to his new home. "The ghosts may still be here."

Jason had burst into the police station ten minutes ago, screaming that ghosts had haunted him right out of Usher House, a big, fancy mansion on the outskirts of town. Jason had purchased Usher House last year. He had wanted to tear down the old mansion to build a shopping mall. But the town council had declared Usher House to be a historical landmark. Since he couldn't do anything else with it, Jason finally moved into the place just last week.

The detectives rushed over to Usher House.

Weird noises could be heard coming from the old place. It sounded as if the house was moaning. The noise went on for a few moments before finally stopping.

Now the three were gathered together on the porch, about to enter the dark and creepy house.

Inside, the house was pitch black, except for the light given off by three candles set in individual holders on a nearby table. The flames flickered as the threesome entered, the draft creating dancing images on the highly polished candlesticks.

Deductive Dog grabbed one candlestick off the spotless table, handing another to his partner, Cat.

"Be careful," Dog warned. "Watch those flames in this old house."

"And watch out for those spirits," said Jason.

The trio began searching the house for ghosts.

"It all started in here," Jason said.

He led them through some double doors into a library. Books of all sorts normally filled these dusty shelves, but now the room was a wreck. Papers were everywhere, books had been tossed all about, and even a small set of shelves had been pushed over.

"I don't see any ghosts," Dog whispered.

"They're here, all right," said Jason. The candlelight etched his face with deep shadows. "I feel them all around us."

"Why don't you tell us what happened," said Dog.

"I was in the library, working late. I keep the lights off to save on electricity, so I use candles. I find it kind of romantic. All those old books, the soft glow of candlelight, the quiet solitude . . ."

"If we can focus on these ghosts," Dog grumbled.

"Oh, sorry. I had lit these candles and put them on my table. After about an hour, I began to hear a strange moaning sound. When I went to investigate, books flew off the shelf at me. A strong wind whirled into the room. It picked me up and tossed me into the hall. That's when I ran out of the house."

"Whatever was here seems to be gone now," Dog said.

"The council will have to let me tear this place down now," said Jason. "They won't want to have a real haunted house around. There's no telling what might happen with these ghosts on the loose."

"I'm not worried," Cat whispered to Dog. "It shouldn't be too hard to shed some light on this ghost story."

WHAT CLUE DOES CAT HAVE?

Once you solve this case, find all the ghosts that are haunting the library.

Answer on page 62

Illustrated by R. Michael Palan

M Is for Monsters

At least thirty objects in this picture begin with the letter *M*. How many can you find?

Illustrated by Joe Seidita

Lucky List

You'll be lucky if you can unscramble these words. All the items below are superstitions, considered to bring either good luck or bad luck.

DOGO	**ABD**
ORUF-EFAL VERLOC	PETSPING NO WALEDISK SCARCK
BOSHNEWI	NEPO LUMBERLA DESINI
BITBAR'S TOOF	KLAW DENRU DERDAL
FECA-PU NYNEP	CACKERD RIMROR
ROSHESOHSE	CLAKB STAC
GHOSTINO RATS	PILESLD LAST

Illustrated by Liisa Chauncy Guida

Answer on page 62

Row, Row, Row

Each pumpkin has something in common with the two others in the same row. For example, in the top row across, each pumpkin has a triangular nose. Look at the other rows across, down, and diagonally. Can you tell what each row of pumpkins has in common?

Answer on page 62

Illustrated by Jerry Zimmerman

Egg Hunt

There are dozens of eggs hidden in this picture.
How many can you find?

Illustrated by Lynn Adams

Adventures in the Night

This house looks friendly, but in the cellar
Lurks a mean and nasty feller
Who plans to ruin Halloween
For every child, adult, and teen.
When trick-or-treaters all feel dandy,
He'll jump out to grab their candy.
But now the kids can spoil his plan
If only they can cross the land.
To help catch this creep, simply say
What objects they'll find along the way:
Apple, candle, spider, hat,
Jack-o'-lantern, then a cat,
An owl, a crown, broom, and bat.
Once confronted, the sneak will scat,
The candy's recovered and that's that.

The path is clear on page 63.

Illustrated by Charles Jordan

October Items

Some of these facts are true and some are false.
It's up to you to separate the tricks from the treats.

1. October is considered National Car Care Month, National Clock Month, National Computer Learning Month, and National Cosmetology Month.
2. **Father-in-law Day is in October.**
3. Jesse Jackson, Brett Favre, Neve Campbell, Richard Dreyfuss, Margaret Thatcher, and Pat Sajak were all born in October.
4. **Jack-o'-lanterns were believed to keep evil spirits away from homes.**
5. Mount Rushmore was completed in October 1941.
6. **The Super Bowl is usually played in October.**
7. The Druids of ancient England believed that October marked the end of the year.

The truth is revealed on page 63.

Illustrated by John Manders

Costume Parade

Follow the leader of this fantastic parade and find the paintbrush, banana, heart, block, mouse, lizard, egg, hamburger, scissors, parrot, butterfly, pear, swan, cupcake, washer, sock, man in the moon, and dog's head.

Illustrated by Carol Sutherby

Halloween banners illustrated by Jeff Shelly

Transylvania

When you go trick-or-treating here, you've got to make sure you know all the right castles! We're in Transylvania, a historic region in the eastern European country of Romania and home of Dracula, the legendary vampire. Once a part of Hungary, Transylvania was invaded by Romanians in World War I. It was later made an official part of Romania as part of a peace settlement in 1920.

Though it has a very scary reputation, the name Transylvania can be translated to mean "beyond the woods."

The area has become linked in legend with such creatures as vampires, mainly because of Bram Stoker's famous horror tale, *Dracula*. The character of Dracula was based on a real-life Transylvanian prince named Vlad Tepesh. He was also called "The Impaler" because of the way he treated his enemies.

Today, people travel to Transylvania to explore its many castles and walk its historic countryside. Most travelers consider it a very interesting place to visit—in the daytime!

Illustrated by Tom Powers

Transylvania Polka

Dare to connect these dots and watch what materializes.

Waltz to page 63 for the answer.

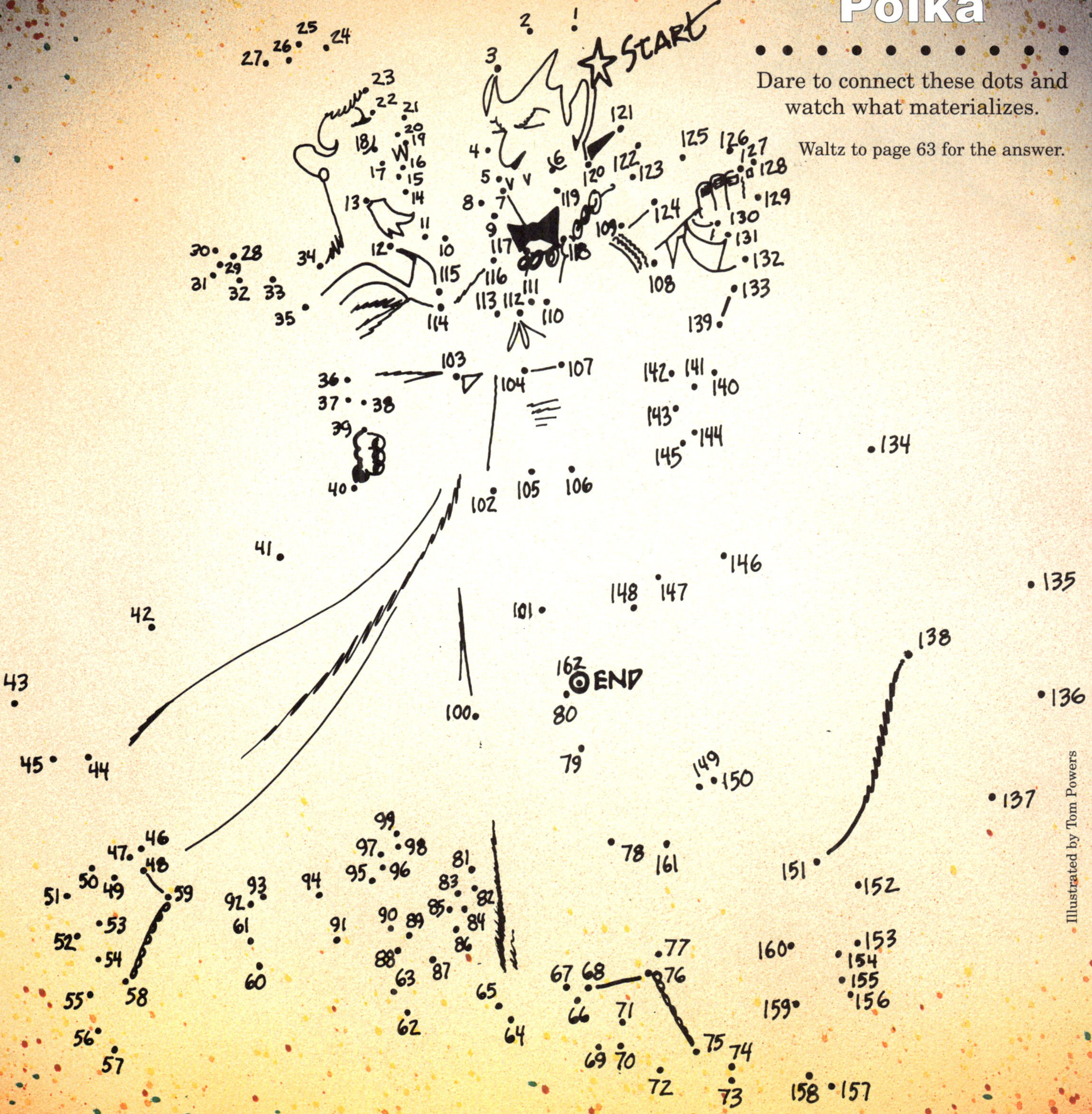

Illustrated by Tom Powers

Mansion of Mystery

Many treasure hunters have tried to spend a night in the spooky old King mansion, searching for its vast hidden fortune. Starting at the front door, follow the directions and gather the letters in the proper sequence. These will lead you to the treasure and will tell you what is hidden in the locked trunk.

1. Before going in, take the letter from the door knocker. Now look for the grandfather clock.
2. Take the letter from the clock. Head upstairs to the red room.
3. You want the letter on the pillow. Now get something to eat.
4. Open the refrigerator slowly for the next letter. Head into the garden.
5. The letter you're after is growing from that mound. Go up the kitchen stairs.
6. Along the way, pull the letter from the second painting.
7. In the attic, the spiders have the letter you want.
8. Outside on the roof is where the next letter is shining. Be careful!
9. Back inside, the library has the next letter you need. Take the yellow one.
10. As you pull that letter, a secret panel swings open to reveal the treasure. Look straight in to find the last letter.
11. To uncover what's in the waiting chest, take the letters you've collected and read them backwards.

Answer on page 63

Illustrated by Liisa Chauncy

I
M
O
C
F
O
P
C
H
W
O
B
Y
D
N

Kooky Spooks

How many differences can you find between these two pictures?

Illustrated by Bill Basso

One Dark and Stormy Night

At last! Dr. Karloff's greatest experiment is finished and ready to be released on the world. Is it a scary caterpillar creature or a triple-decker peanut butter, liverwurst, and pickle sandwich? Or something even more horrible? Use your imagination to draw in what you think Dr. Karloff has been working on.

Illustrated by Bill Basso

FALL FOUL-UP

Ah, 'tis autumn, bringing with it brightly colored leaves, pumpkin pies, apple cider, surfing at the beach . . . surfing at the beach? What's going on here? See if you can find what's out of season in this fall picture.

Illustrated by Ben Tyler

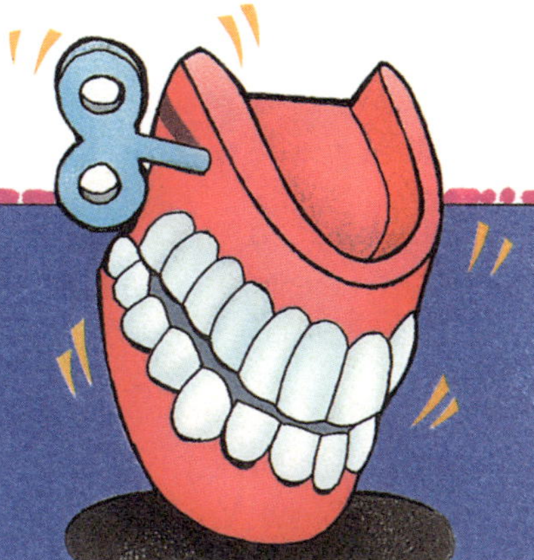

CHUCKLES and CHILLS

1. What do you call a frankfurter with no meat in it?

2. What food is never part of a vampire's diet?

3. What do monsters eat for supper?

4. How did the monster get in the house?

5. What's a mummy's favorite game show?

6. What do polite vampires say to their victims?

7. What did one Halloween candle say to the other Halloween candle?

Invisible boy: I just took a test in school. There were twenty questions and I left them all blank.

Invisible mom: So what did you get?

Invisible boy: 100%, of course!

Publisher: I need a spooky story. Do you know anyone who could help me?

Editor: My friend is just the guy you want.

Publisher: Why him?

Editor: He's a ghost writer.

Al: I can't afford a costume this year.

Sal: Don't worry, you can still go to the masquerade party.

Al: As what?

Sal: The Invisible Man.

Illustrated by Terry Sirrell

Pam: Did you hear about the new musical group called The Mummies?

Sam: No, what kind of music do they play?

Pam: Wrap!

8. Why did the principal hire the ghost?

9. Why won't the Invisible Man look in the closet?

Answers on page 63

Guess Who

A mystery person can be found in the boxes on the next page. Two of the characters he created can also be found there.

This person was born in New York City. This person was an essayist, historian, and one of the first of America's great writers. Some of this person's famous works were inspired by stories and legends told by Dutch descendants living in New York. This mystery person, using the pen name Diedrich Knickerbocker, wrote a history of New York. This book brought the word *Knickerbocker* into the English language. This mystery person is buried in Sleepy Hollow Cemetery.

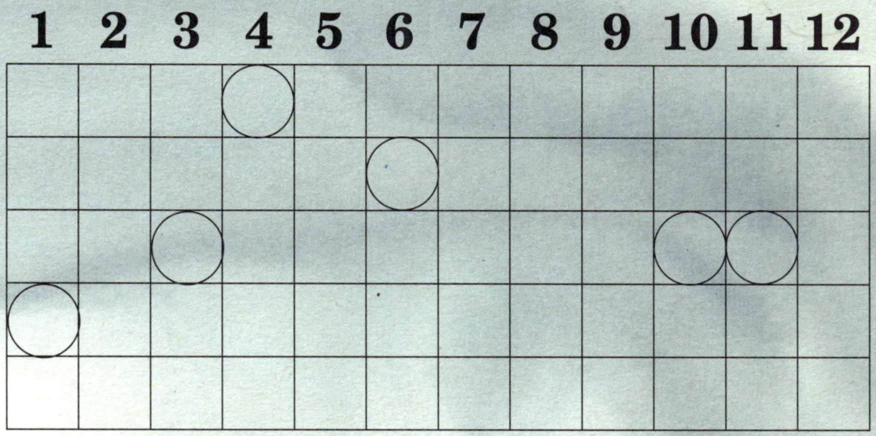

To solve this puzzle, write the five-letter answer to each clue vertically in the corresponding number column.

When complete, and if done correctly, one character's name will be spelled out across the top row, and a second character's name will be spelled out across the bottom row. The author's last name will appear in the circles, reading from left to right.

1. Plural form of *radius*
2. Sir ________ Newton
3. Horizontal rod or branch that birds stand on
4. A stringed instrument slightly larger than a violin
5. In acting, to make up and perform something on the spur of the moment
6. ________glycerin is used in making dynamite.
7. Book title: *Around the ________ in Eighty Days*
8. Of or like an ion
9. Not ever
10. Nairobi is the capital of this country.
11. Boston airport
12. To wipe out

Answer on page 63

Illustrated by Judith Hunt

That's the Spirit

How many ghosts can you find haunting this scene?

Illustrated by Joe Seidita

Mummy Maze

Morton the Mummy has forgotten the secret passage to his royal chamber. Can you help him find his way back?

Illustrated by Gregg Valley

Answer on page 63

Daze of the Month

This calendar page may look silly, but it holds the answer to a very important riddle. Follow the clues from date to date to find the letters mentioned. Put each letter into the space whose number is given in each clue, and you'll come up with the answer in no time.

- Octember 32 holds letter number nine.
- Find letter four on the second Thursday.
- Smash Wednesday will give you letter one.
- Letter five is featured on the day of the afternoon solstice.
- Harbor Day has letter six.
- The third Tuesday after the second Monday has letter ten.
- St. Hat Trick's Day, honoring the hockey player who chased all the snakes out of Madison Square Garden, has letter seven.
- The date of the blue moon holds letter two.
- Letter eight can be found on Garbage Day.
- Dependence Day will give you letter three.

Why are Saturday and Sunday so limp?

1 2 3 4 ' 5 3   1 2 3   6 3 3 7   3 8 9 10.

Answer on page 63

Illustrated by Susanne Demarco

OCTEMBER
1 A
2 J
3 Q
4 Dependence Day E
5 U
6 V
7 C
8 G
9 Harbor Day W
10
11
12 Y
13 Bad Friday
14 L
15 M
16 X
17 Sarah's Birthday B
18 Smash Wednesday T
19
20
21 Garbage Day N
22 St. Hat Trick's Day K
23
24 Passunder ends S
25 I
26 Frank's giving Z
27
28 P
29 Afternoon Solstice R
30
31 F
32 D
33
34 Blue Moon H
35

Phone Fun

On a telephone, each number 2 through 9 can stand for three different letters. For example, the 2 could stand for *A*, *B*, or *C*. See if you can call up the answer to the code below by punching in the right letters.

9 4 2 8' 7   8 4 3   2 3 7 8   9 2 9

8 6   8 2 5 5   8 6   2   6 6 6 7 8 3 7?

2 9   5 6 6 4   3 4 7 8 2 6 2 3!

Illustrated by Belinda Lyon

Answer on page 63

Ghoul Grid

There are thirty-three magical monsters and personalities hiding in the letters below. Don't be afraid to see how many you can find. You can capture them by circling their names in the grid and then crossing them off the list. Look up, down, across, backward, and diagonally, because they may be hiding anywhere.

BANSHEES
BOGYMAN
CREATURES
DEMONS
DRAGON
DWARF
ELVES
FAIRIES
GARGOYLE
GENIE
GHOSTS
GHOUL
GIANT
GNOME
GOLEM
GREMLIN
HARPY
HAUNTS
HOBGOBLIN
IMPS
JACK FROST
LEPRECHAUNS
MONSTER
OGRES
PHANTASM
PHANTOMS
PIXIE
POLTERGEIST
ROCS
SANDMAN
SPECTER
TROLL
WISPS

A	J	O	G	R	E	S	E	N	F	R	A	W	D
M	D	A	X	H	G	C	F	A	I	R	I	E	S
S	P	R	C	I	O	D	E	M	O	N	S	P	N
A	O	C	A	K	L	U	R	Y	G	G	E	H	U
T	L	N	R	G	F	M	L	G	N	H	E	A	A
N	T	E	H	E	O	R	I	O	O	O	H	N	H
A	E	F	N	N	A	N	O	B	M	S	S	T	C
H	R	G	S	A	G	T	G	S	E	T	N	O	E
P	G	T	P	C	M	O	U	R	T	S	A	M	R
G	E	N	I	E	B	D	L	R	E	N	B	S	P
R	I	I	M	L	Z	L	N	E	E	M	U	N	E
O	S	P	I	X	I	E	L	A	M	S	L	A	L
C	T	N	W	I	S	P	S	O	S	R	P	I	H
S	E	V	L	E	L	Y	O	G	R	A	G	M	N
H	A	R	P	Y	T	S	P	E	C	T	E	R	I

Answer on page 63

Illustrated by John Nez

Row, Row, Row

Each of these scarecrows has something in common with the two others in the same row. For example, all three scarecrows in the top row across are wearing red hats. Look at the other rows across, down, and diagonally. What's alike in each row?

Illustrated by John Nez

Answer on page 63

Owl Find You

How many owls are hiding in this picture?

Illustrated by Tom Powers

Laboratory Labyrinth

Dr. Zarkoff is up to his old tricks. To add the final ingredient to his energy shake, he's dropping this grape into the beaker. See if you can follow the tubes around to let the doctor know where the grape will end up. Hint: In Dr. Zarkoff's maze, a funnel will catch any grape dropped into it, and the grape will then continue on.

Illustrated by Marc Nadel

Answer on page 63

Bats in the Belfry

Barney is going bats looking up his family tree. Help him find these thirty words that have to do with bats. They're hidden somewhere in the letters on the next page. These words could be anywhere, so look up, down, across, backward, and diagonally in the grid. Once you've found them all, see how many loose bats you can find flying around. Circle BAT as many times as you can find it in this puzzle.

Brown	Greater	Navigate
Caves	Hang	Nectar
Chiroptera	Hibernate	Nocturnal
Ears	Hoary	Red
Echo	Insects	Senses
Flight	Lesser	Silver
Flying Fox	Long Lives	Smell
Friendly	Mammal	Sonar
Fruit Bat	Migrate	Vampire
Good Luck	Muzzle	Wings

Illustrated by Rich Johnson

Answer on page 64

A	N	T	A	B	A	R	E	T	P	O	R	I	H	C	K
B	W	I	N	G	S	T	T	R	Q	T	S	A	F	T	C
S	O	S	O	N	A	R	A	L	A	E	N	F	R	A	U
T	R	I	Y	G	R	T	N	B	S	G	K	L	I	B	L
C	B	L	I	R	C	S	R	N	A	S	T	I	E	R	D
E	T	V	B	E	B	B	E	R	E	T	A	G	N	D	O
S	A	E	N	A	A	S	B	V	E	L	B	H	D	E	O
N	B	R	T	T	T	A	I	C	A	B	Z	T	L	R	G
I	T	E	S	E	T	L	H	M	B	C	A	Z	Y	I	S
J	I	S	V	R	G	O	M	T	A	B	A	T	U	P	M
B	U	S	P	N	A	A	A	E	T	A	R	G	I	M	E
A	R	E	O	R	M	B	N	O	C	T	U	R	N	A	L
T	F	L	Y	I	N	G	F	O	X	S	T	A	B	V	L

Spelling Trouble

Strega the Sorceress is stirring up a special brew. But she's so excited, her words are coming out all jumbled. See if you can straighten the words in her spell so everything will come out right.

Answer on page 64

Illustrated by Terry Rogers

Halloween and Vine

These pictures are out of order. Can you number them to show what happened first, second, and so on?

Answer on page 64

Illustrated by Barbara Gray

CAT & DOG MYSTERY

CASE #130
The Costume Party Caper

Deductive Dog and Clue Cat had been invited to one of the swankiest affairs of the season. Fifi La Feline was throwing her annual charity costume ball, and the detectives were on security duty. At 11:03 p.m., the party was in full swing. The music was loud, and everyone was having a good time—everyone except the hostess.

The butler came to ask the detectives to pull themselves away from the buffet table. Dog and Cat followed the butler into a room where Fifi La Feline was crying.

"What's wrong?" asked Dog.

"My original Picattso painting has been stolen," Fifi wailed. "It was absolutely priceless. I can't believe it's gone. And my hand-painted purple Italian vase is shattered!" Fifi threw herself on the couch and continued to sob.

"Where was the painting?" Dog shouted above the noise of the band, trying to get Fifi to focus on the problem.

"Upstairs in the hallway, across from my bedroom. It hung above the table that my beautiful vase used to stand on." Fifi buried her head in the long black cape of her costume and let out a long wail.

"When did you last see this painting?" Dog asked.

"It was there before the party started," Fifi said. "But when I just went up to check my answering machine, I noticed it was gone!"

Deductive Dog and Clue Cat exchanged glances before climbing the stairs together. The noise from the party floated up behind them, still loud even on the second floor.

At the scene of the crime, they stepped carefully around all the broken pieces of purple pottery. Suddenly, Deductive Dog spotted an important piece of evidence.

"Look, the culprit must have dropped this handkerchief. It has the initials Q. Z. sewn onto it."

"Ouch," Cat said. He looked down at one foot. A piece of clear glass was stuck in his wounded paw.

"Be careful," said Dog. "The purple glass from this broken vase is everywhere."

As Cat pulled out the clear shard, he said, "We just have to find the one guest at Fifi's party who has the initials Q. Z. and the case is solved." He then put the shard in his pocket as a possible clue.

Back downstairs, the detectives asked Fifi which guest might have dropped the handkerchief. Fifi then pointed out three different costumes: Quincy Zimmer was dressed as a fish in a bowl, Queenie Zee looked like a tiny fairy, and Quadro Zenith had come as a mummy.

"Unbelievable," Dog said as he slapped himself in the head. "Three guests with the initials Q. Z. It's never easy, is it, Cat?"

"We'll need to talk to each of them," Cat said.

Fifi agreed to let the detectives use her study. She then went out to the party and sent the three guests in. Quadro Zenith was the first to arrive, followed by a fish and a fairy.

"Why are we here?" demanded the fairy, squinting up at the detectives. "I was just about to dance with that handsome dragonfly."

Dog looked over each suspect. "A crime has been committed. And you three have been called in because a handkerchief with the initials Q. Z. was found at the scene of the crime."

"The only time I could've lost my handkerchief was when I checked my pocket watch at 10:30." With that, Quadro Zenith pulled out a big pocket watch that had a broken crystal face.

"Well, where's your handkerchief?" Cat asked.

Quadro's face turned red. "I can't seem to find it. I must have lost it somewhere during the dance."

"What crime was committed, anyway?" Queenie asked.

"Someone took Fifi's Picattso painting," Cat answered.

This set Fifi to crying louder than ever. Queenie Zee took off from the couch to fly over to comfort her feline friend. Unfortunately, Queenie misjudged the distance and flew into the lamp instead.

"Are you all right?" Fifi asked.

"Yes, I just couldn't see without my glasses."

"Why aren't you wearing them?" Dog asked.

"Oh, some clumsy gnu gnocked, I mean knocked, them off my head during the hokey-pokey contest. They got stepped on. See?"

With that, Queenie held up the trampled spectacles.

"I didn't even carry a handkerchief tonight," Quincy Zimmer said through a crack in his fish bowl. "So I couldn't have done it."

"Well, one of you did," Dog said. "And you spoiled the party for everyone else."

"Not to mention my Halloween," Cat said. "And that's one trick that is no treat."

With that, Cat put the cuffs on one suspect.

Can you tell which guest took the painting?

Now scour the big picture to find all fifteen crooks who helped remove the painting.

The case is solved on page 64.

Illustrated by R. Michael Palan

Brainstorm Brian's

Handy Dandy Treat Handler

Instead of trick-or-treating, Brainstorm Brian decides to let his costume do all the work. Brian pushes clothesline (A), and Ghost (B) swoops along, frightening frog (C). Frog leaps onto platform, which pulls up dustpan (D), tipping over cauldron (E). Chocolate syrup (F) pours out, breaking spider web (G), thus releasing clapper of alarm clock (H), allowing it to ring. Witch (I) is reminded that it is witching hour and grabs broom (J), kicking up dust (K), causing dragon (L) to sneeze fire. As marshmallows (M) get toasted, bat (N) jumps up and down excitedly, flinging jack-o'-lantern (O) onto device, which pulls up rope (P), causing skeleton (Q) to dance. Rattling bones spook black cat (R), which crosses path of baker (S), causing him to drop doughnuts (T) due to bad luck. As one doughnut falls on lever (U), hook releases bag (V), which catches tumbling crullers as it is pulled up by spring (W). And so, Brian's treats are delivered to him. That's a pretty neat trick!

Illustrated by Marc Nadel

In the Bag

It's All Hallow's Eve, the night for tricks and treats. You've spent all week making your costume just right. And now you think you're ready to head out and grab some goodies.

But not so fast, Svengali!

Sure, your costume looks great, but what about that bag? Would a princess carry a paltry pillowcase? Would an astronaut keep his candy in a paper bag? Would some superhero stash snacks in a simple sack? No!

All the best costumes require just the right accessory in which to keep your tasty treats. Check out these suggestions for terrific totes.

Pizza Boxes

Glue together a pile of empty pizza boxes. Then cut a circle out of the center of the inner boxes so that you have a secret hole. When you go to the door, the trick will be that the people think they've ordered ten pizzas! When you reveal that they don't have to pay for them all, they'll gladly give you treats to put inside your boxes.

The Addams Family

If you're going out as one of the Addams clan, get a shoe box. Cover it in black paper. Cut a hole in the bottom of the box so that you can slip your hand through. Tape one of the short ends of the box top to act as a hinge. Attach a string to the other end so that you can pull the top open with your other hand. Then carry the box around with you. When the unsuspecting homeowner offers you candy, pull the lid open so that Thing comes out to grab the goodies. That way you get two characters instead of one.

Fire Fighter

A big helmet, a yellow raincoat, a piece of garden hose, and some boots make a great fire fighter. But where to hide the snacks? How about in a fire hydrant? Get a big drum carton from oatmeal cereal or popcorn. Cover it with red paper. Add a top from paper-mâché, or place a margarine container upside down on the top of the carton. Decorate it to look like a fire hydrant. Pull the top off and put the candy inside.

Bank Bags

A pillowcase can be turned into an old-time bank bag by adding a few lines to make the symbol for money. It makes the perfect bag for a police officer or a security guard.

Illustrated by Judith Hunt

Row, Row, Row

It's Manny Monster's birthday and all of his friends have gathered for a party. Each monster has something in common with the two other monsters in the same row. For example, all of the monsters in the top row across have two triangular fangs. Look at the other rows across, down, and diagonally. What's the same about each row of three?

Illustrated by Lynn Adams

Answer on page 64

Snooperstition

It might be bad luck to do this puzzle while stepping on a banana peel. But it might be good luck to do this puzzle while thinking of a hippopotamus. Superstitions are signs that people believe have to do with luck. Try to find all the symbols of good or bad luck in this picture. Good luck!

The luck is revealed on page 64.

Illustrated by Leslie Harris

ANSWERS

MONSTER MASH (pages 4-5)
Why do grave diggers make excellent storytellers?
BECAUSE THEY DIG UP GOOD PLOTS

ROW, ROW, ROW (page 6)

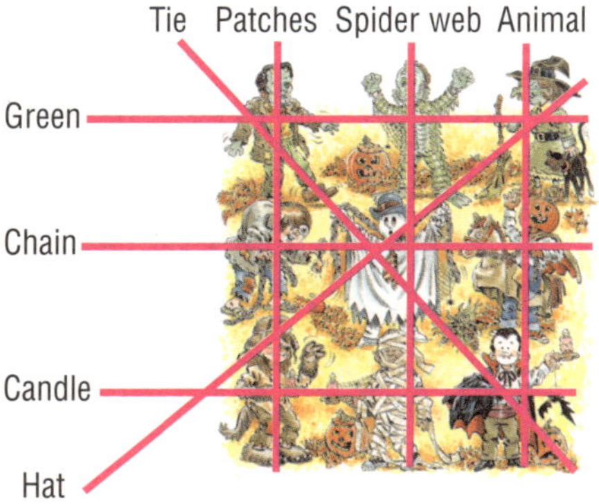

DON'T BE AFRAID (page 7)

B	G	O	T	R	I	C	K	O	R	T	R	E	A	T
G	H	O	U	L	S	E	M	U	T	S	O	C	C	J
G	O	B	L	I	N	S	U	A	J	W	O	L	F	K
O	S	C	A	R	Y	I	L	Z	Y	P	E	E	R	C
O	T	B	N	E	W	T	O	R	H	L	A	R	G	A
D	S	L	V	B	C	O	L	W	U	D	X	E	B	L
S	H	C	A	N	D	Y	M	A	E	R	C	S	E	B
N	W	G	E	O	M	A	S	K	L	E	F	M	E	S
I	A	S	G	N	E	T	Y	W	E	L	T	O	A	R
K	O	T	N	E	E	W	O	L	L	A	H	O	O	E
P	L	A	A	E	I	H	A	P	H	N	G	R	L	T
M	E	B	R	C	L	F	U	N	H	Z	I	B	H	S
U	T	O	O	C	N	W	A	L	H	V	N	E	J	N
P	B	C	L	S	E	H	C	T	I	W	E	M	C	O
S	T	A	C	H	A	N	H	A	E	N	N	O	O	M

PETER, PETER, PUMPKIN POSER (pages 10-11)

MUMMY'S THE WORD (page 12)

A—2 C—1
B—3 D—4

WHAT'S IN A WORD? (page 13)
Here are some of the words we found. You may have found others.

ale	halo	lawn	own
all	heal	lean	wall
allow	heel	Leo	wan
alone	hen	loan	wane
anew	hew	lone	wean
awe	hewn	low	well
awl	hole	new	whale
eel	hone	noel	wheel
eon	how	now	when
ewe	howl	one	whoa
hale	lane	owe	whole
hallow	law	owl	won

FRIGHT SIGHTS (pages 18-19)
The professor is wearing his letter sweater, eye tie, and more than one blue shoes.

The rhymes shown by the ghost host include:

frightening lightning
squeaker sneaker
pants dance
book hook
fat bat
scary canary
rich witch
hobblin' goblin
dead Fred
scare chair
bone phone
mummy tummy
moose noose
lime slime
black crack

LOST IN THE CASTLE (page 20)
You should use door number 5.
9 + 24 = 33; 33 - 16 = 17;
17 + 3 = 20; 20 ÷ 4 = 5

CAT & DOG MYSTERY (pages 22-23)

CASE #222—THE HAUNTED LIBRARY
Jason Jackal claimed that the candles were burning for longer than an hour. Yet when the group came into the house, there was just a little wax on the candlesticks and none on the table. When confronted by the detectives, Jackal admitted that his story was all part of a scheme to get the town to allow him to tear the Usher House down.

LUCKY LIST (page 25)

GOOD
four-leaf clover
wishbone
rabbit's foot
face-up penny
horseshoes
shooting star

BAD
stepping on sidewalk cracks
open umbrella inside
walk under ladder
cracked mirror
black cats
spilled salt

ROW, ROW, ROW (page 26)

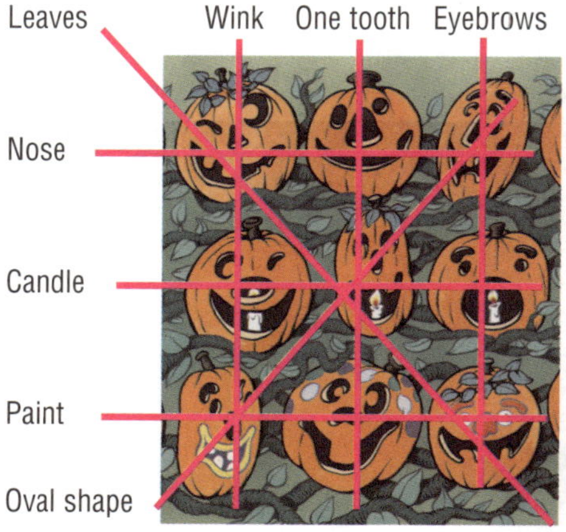

ADVENTURES IN THE NIGHT
(pages 28-29)

OCTOBER ITEMS (page 30)
Number 2 and number 6 are incorrect. Mother-in-law Day is in October, and the Super Bowl is usually played in January.

TRANSYLVANIA POLKA
(page 33)

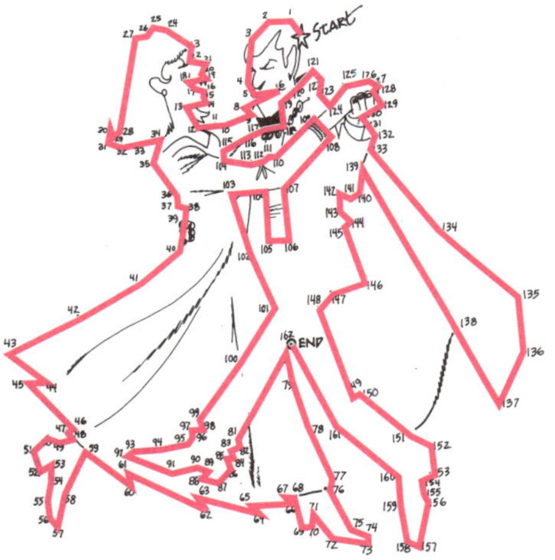

MANSION OF MYSTERY
(pages 34-35)
If you've followed the directions correctly, you've found COMIC BOOKS.

CHUCKLES AND CHILLS
(page 39)

1. A Hallow-weeny
2. Steaks
3. Ghoul-ash and grave-y
4. With a skeleton key
5. *Name That Tomb*
6. "Fangs a lot!"
7. "You look wicked tonight."
8. To give his school more spirit
9. Because he can never find anything to wear!

GUESS WHO (pages 40-41)

1	2	3	4	5	6	7	8	9	10	11	12
R	I	P	V	A	N	W	I	N	K	L	E
A	S	E	I	D	I	O	O	E	E	O	R
D	A	R	O	L	T	R	N	V	N	G	A
I	A	C	L	I	R	L	I	E	Y	A	S
I	C	H	A	B	O	D	C	R	A	N	E

Rip Van Winkle and Ichabod Crane are two characters created by Washington Irving.

MUMMY MAZE (page 43)

DAZE OF THE MONTH
(pages 44-45)
Why are Saturday and Sunday so limp?
THEY'RE THE WEEK (WEAK) ENDS.

PHONE FUN (page 46)
WHAT'S THE BEST WAY TO TALK TO A MONSTER?
BY LONG DISTANCE!

GHOUL GRID (page 47)

A	J	O	G	R	E	S	E	N	F	R	A	W	D
M	D	A	X	H	G	C	F	A	I	R	I	E	S
S	P	R	C	I	O	D	E	M	O	N	S	P	N
A	O	C	A	K	L	U	R	Y	G	G	E	H	U
T	L	N	R	G	F	M	L	G	N	H	E	A	A
N	T	E	H	E	O	R	I	O	O	O	H	N	H
A	E	F	N	N	A	N	O	B	M	S	S	T	C
H	R	G	S	A	G	T	G	S	E	T	N	O	E
P	G	T	P	C	M	O	U	R	T	S	A	M	R
G	E	N	I	E	B	D	L	R	E	N	B	S	P
R	I	I	M	L	Z	L	N	E	E	M	U	N	E
O	S	P	I	X	I	E	L	A	M	S	L	A	L
C	T	N	W	I	S	P	S	O	S	R	P	I	H
S	E	V	L	E	L	Y	O	G	R	A	G	M	N
H	A	R	P	Y	T	S	P	E	C	T	E	R	I

ROW, ROW, ROW (page 48)

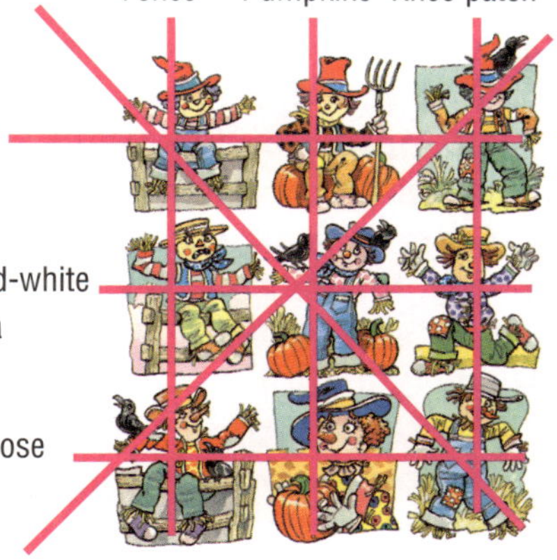

LABORATORY LABYRINTH
(pages 50-51)

BATS IN THE BELFRY
(pages 52-53)

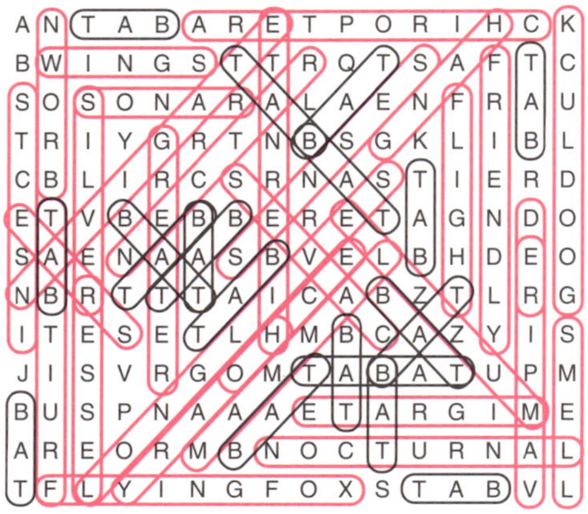

There are twenty-one "BAT"s flying loose.

SPELLING TROUBLE (page 54)
First a cup of warts from a **frog**,
Then a **pinch** of hair **from** a hog.
Two drops of bat **blood**,
A half **pound** of dried **mud**.
Some **sugar** for taste,
Be careful, don't **waste**.
Boil it, **shake** it,
Turn it **over** and **bake** it.
Next, let it **cool**
Till it **starts** to **drool**.
Then **throw** on black **icing**
So it's **ready** for **slicing**.
And that's the **way** you **make**
A witch's **birthday** cake!

HALLOWEEN AND VINE
(page 55)

5	3
6	1
2	4

CAT & DOG MYSTERY
(pages 56-57)

CASE #130—
THE COSTUME PARTY CAPER
If you check the clear glass shard in Clue Cat's hand, you'll see it matches the piece that is missing from Queenie Zee's eyeglasses in the top left corner. The detectives were tipped off to Queenie's eye problem when she flew into the lamp. Queenie confessed that the painting had proven to be heavier than she expected. When Queenie pulled the painting off the wall, she was knocked back into the purple vase. Her glasses then flew off and broke. Next, Queenie called for help, and all her worker bees showed up to cart off the painting.

Fifteen bees are still at the party. Did you find them all?

ROW, ROW, ROW (page 60)

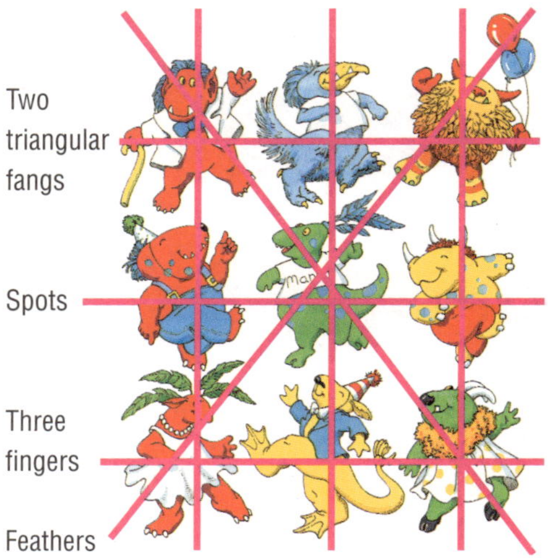

SNOOPERSTITION (page 61)
GOOD LUCK
fingers crossed
horseshoe
salt over shoulder
four-leaf clover
wishbone
BAD LUCK
cracked mirror
Friday the 13th
walk under the ladder
number 13
black cat
stepping on a crack
umbrella open indoors